I0505521

Make Money Online

Your Guide on How to Get Rich With Information Products

2nd Edition

By Rob Branson

ISBN: 9798606756087
Published by ZML Corp LLC

Table of Contents

DISCLAIMER

This book is written for informational purposes only. This book should be used in the making of an informed decision only. The publisher and author shall have neither liability nor responsibility to any person or entity with respect to any financial loss or damage caused or alleged to be caused directly or indirectly by this book.

This book can be very helpful teaching you ways to make money online, however I make no guarantees that you will actually make any money. Results are not typical. It is just a useful guide with much researched information on ways to make money online.

Earnings and income representations made by Rob Branson are aspirational statements only of your earnings potential. The success of Rob Branson, testimonials and other examples used are exceptional, non-typical results and are not intended to be a guarantee that you or others will achieve the same results. Individual results will always vary and yours will depend entirely on your individual capacity, work ethic, business skills and experience, level of motivation, diligence in applying the information laid out in the Unknownwealth book, the economy, the normal and unforeseen risks of doing business, and other factors. Rob Branson and ZML Corp LLC have no affiliation to Patrick King, Eben Pagen, or Frank Kern, and these names are just used as examples of successful practitioners of selling information products.

ZML Corp LLC and Rob Branson individually, are not responsible for your actions. You are solely responsible for your own moves and decisions and the evaluation and use of our products and services should be based on your own due diligence. You agree that ZML Corp LLC and Rob Branson are not liable to you in any way for your results in using our products and services.

ZML Corp LLC, including Rob Branson personally, may receive compensation for products and services they recommend to you.

Introduction

In this book, we will be going over what I believe is truly the secret to generating wealth on the internet. What makes this method of generating wealth so impressive is the residual income it brings. I would compare it to renting out real estate properties or selling music, except better. Unlike a real job, you do the work once, and then are able to reap the benefits from it forever. Each product you sell builds on the next, which all end up becoming residual income making machines. Aside from the marketing, it becomes a hands-off process. However if you have the proper marketing in place, that can be hands off as well.

This is not a "get rich quick scheme." That's not to say you can't get rich quick though. This will take work on your end and a lot of learning, but if you are motivated and work hard, it will pay off generously for you; I promise. I really try to make everything clear and simple in this book, providing you with all the info and tools to become successful yourself. There are many people (who I will bring up in this book) who have gotten extremely wealthy from the methods I am about to show you. I won't keep you in suspense any longer, so without further ado, let's learn more about the secret which I call "Unknown Wealth."

CHAPTER 1
The Secret to Online Wealth

I'm going to put it out in the open right here for you in the first sentence of Chapter 1; the secret to generating wealth online are information products. Unlike a regular business, there is no brick and motor store which you need to pay for, no inventory you need to keep track of, no employees to hire and no physical product you have to buy. It's a business that is extremely affordable to get into, and can produce a great deal of income if ran effectively.

I've found the most success with one information product in particular, and that is eBooks. Ebooks are a multi-billion dollar industry and there are quite a few people who have become millionaires from them. Look up names like Eben Pagan (Double Your Dating) and Frank Kern (Teach Your Parrot to Talk), and you'll see the results for yourself.

In this book, I will be teaching you how to write, sell and market an eBook, from start to finish. In the bonus chapter, I then show you how to expand on your eBook, and bridge into other information products such as video courses and audiobooks. Here's what we will be going over:

1. How to Come Up With an eBook Idea

2. How to Write Your eBook

3. How to Sell Your eBook

4. How to Market Your eBook

I plan on showing you not just the methods I use, but also the methods of other eBook gurus. This way you can make an informed decision for yourself on the way you want to proceed. I will also be going over other information products you can sell in the last chapter.

What information products such as eBooks allow is something called passive or residual income. What this means is income continues to come in even after all the work (writing the eBook) is completed. The book sit on the shelves, aka the internet, and can continue being sold forever. Income is generated day in and day out, even while you sleep. Unlike a regular job, you don't have to continue working once you write the book. You can actually start working on more eBooks to begin generating more passive income. Other examples of products that provide residual income are music, movies, and renting real estate.

Something I want to mention is this is not a get rich quick scheme. However, with time, it can generate a great deal of wealth, especially the better you get at it. In the beginning, there is a learning curve and you do need to put in a good deal of work. Once you get a hang of things though and your first eBook begins selling, things get a lot easier. Just like anything else, the more you practice and learn the skill, the better you become. Many people strictly do this part time to add a few dollars to their pocket each week. It's up to you how involved you want to get, however obviously don't quit your day job just yet. You of course need to make sure this is for you and you become profitable before you consider doing this full time.

Note: Links to all the websites I mention during this book can be found on the last page. Due to the special relations I have, the links I provide contain coupon codes which can save you a significant amount of money versus just visiting the site on your own.

As a token of appreciation to my readers, I am offering my special report titled *Amazon Advertising Secrets* **absolutely free!** In this special report, you'll learn my unique Amazon PPC strategy, which allows you to get your book in front of thousands of readers for the least amount of money. Just copy & paste the link below into your browser and put in your email address, and it will immediately be sent to you!

fastlink.xyz/secrets

CHAPTER 2
Getting Started

The first thing you need to do is come up with an eBook idea. For me, my first eBook was on acne. I had terrible acne in high school, but did find a way to finally get rid of it during college. There was so much trial and error for me when it came to getting rid of my acne; so many products I tried that didn't work and so much money wasted. Now let's fast forward to when I graduated from college and had been working crappy jobs for three years. I had a girlfriend at the time who ended breaking up with me. One night, up late searching around the internet, I stumbled upon an eBook titled "The Magic of Making Up" by T Dub Jackson. This eBook promised to get my ex back into my arms for $40. I was quite sad at the time and at a point where I would do anything to have my ex back, so I bought it.

I've been quite entrepreneurial from a young age, so as I was reading the eBook I thought to myself "I could do this with acne." I know so much about acne already with everything I've been through, and could teach others what I know. Right then and there I literally closed out the eBook and began writing my own book. And over the last 7 years, with the same type of trial and error I had to go through to get rid of my acne, I have perfected the art of writing and selling eBooks. I have successfully written and marketed five eBooks up to this date.

So a good place to start writing an eBook is with your own life experiences. But if you don't happen to be an expert in any particular subject, there are other ways to get started which guru Frank Kern proves. Frank Kern, who I mentioned in Chapter 1, is an information product guru with a net worth of over 28 million. He got started with an eBook titled "Teach Your Parrot to Talk." Was he a parrot expert? No not at all. He was on Google searching around one day and noticed (which I'll show you how later) there were a lot of searches for "how to teach your parrot to talk." Seeing the value in this, he hired a parrot specialist to write an eBook on the subject for him. He then began marketing it and that was the start to his career.

There is of course startup costs to this option, as the expert probably won't write the book for free. You could possibly ask that expert to split the profits with you. Considering he or she would write the book, and you would handle all the marketing, it's a pretty easy gig for them. I personally have written all my eBooks myself, however if I saw a hot niche market and knew little about it, I would not hesitate to find an expert in the field. A recent example is the bitcoin craze that is going on. I could definitely see where there could be money made teaching people about bitcoin. Considering I know little about it, an expert in the field to help me would be very beneficial.

Another idea for an eBook to write, though controversial, is to write one similar to an existing eBook out in the market. I am not advising you to plagiarize, as that is illegal. However, if there is an eBook on a subject you're interested in that is already out on the market you can buy it, read it, and then use what you learned to create your own version. This allows for a quick way to get into a niche market. A great website to find a ton of eBooks is called Clickbank (which I'll talk about more later). Besides reading eBooks, you could also read an actual paperback book, or take a video course on a particular subject and then turn that into an eBook.

After you're done writing your book, it's helpful to have a professional editor go over it to correct any of your mistakes, as well as to get a second opinion on the wording of your book. There are two websites where you can find book editors who charge very reasonable fees.

The first website is called Upwork (formerly eLance). Book editors are just one of the services this website offers. Other freelancers for hire include website designers, accountants, virtual customer service agents, and more.

The second website is called Fiverr (**fastlink.xyz/fiver**). Originally this website started out as a place you could go and every service on the website was only $5. Today is has morphed into allowing sellers to offer different prices for their services, however many quality services can still be found for only $5. Here you can also find many book editors to help you. You are able to see which country they are from, reviews, number of projects, etc. This is my go-to website for finding services. You won't believe the stuff you can find on this website. Just to give you an idea, for my Uncle's 50th birthday I hired a guy on Fiverr to make a video juggling knives singing the "happy birthday song" for $5!

One thing to keep in mind with eBooks is the most money can be made in niche markets with low competition. So if you do decide to venture outside your own expertise, look for a book you can sell that fits this criteria.

CHAPTER 3
Selling Your Product

There are two primary ways to sell an eBook. You can either:

Option #1: Sell it on your own website

Option #2: Sell it in an eBook marketplace like Amazon

There are pros and cons to both of these strategies. Some gurus prefer one arena, while others prefer the other; it comes down to personal preference. Let's go over these two strategies now.

Option #1 – Your Own Website

This strategy is key to really making significant wealth with eBooks, in my personal opinion. There is obviously a learning curve of how to build a website, how to market your website, etc. Once you do learn all the necessary skills and everything is set up though, your website will generate income like a well-oiled machine. From start to finish, it took me 6 months to learn how to build a website and get my first eBook selling. While I can't go over every detail of web design in this book, I can take out all the trial and error that I went through to show you the easiest, fastest way to learn and get up and running. Also, I want to mention that a website is not expensive to maintain. You can expect to pay around $120 a year to run it.

The first thing you need to do to start a website is come up with a domain name. You want to obtain a domain name that correlates with your product. It does not need to have the products name in it per se, however it would be ideal if people came across your website and knew what you were selling just from the name. Many catchy website names are already taken, so sometimes you really have to brainstorm to come up with an adequate one. Websites like GoDaddy allow you to type in a domain name to see if it's still available. Domains typically cost about $12 a year. Sometimes you'll see a domain name "for sale" on GoDaddy. These are people who have bought domain names, and then are reselling them at a premium. These can range from $50 to $100,000+. I would highly discourage buying a domain name from a seller, especially in the beginning of your eBook business. I have found it's not worth the premium that is charged. People aren't going to find your website by randomly typing names into their URL bar; they're going to find it with Google searches and ads. So unless the domain is really catchy and fairly inexpensive, as in less than $100, I wouldn't do it.

With websites, you want to buy what is known as a "top level domain." These are the .com, .net, and .org extensions, with .com being the #1 choice. There are a TON of different website extensions these days (.co, .xyz, .business, etc.) however Google looks at top level domain names more favorably. This is important when it comes to search results, which I talk more about in Chapter 4. Also, any domain extension besides .com, .net, or .org can look spammy and low-class to your audience.

Some other tips when buying a domain name is to not make it too long. Try to keep it short and professional. For example, let's say you're writing an eBook on dog training. TrainYourDog.com would be great (though it's probably taken). HowToTrainYourDogEffectively.com is most likely available, but way too long and looks odd to your visitors. I feel the simpler the domain name, the better. Also, dashes look low class in a domain name. How-To-Train-Your-Dog.com does not look as professional as HowToTrainYourDog.com. So while brain storming for a domain name, try to keep dashes out of it. If the only good one you can find includes a dash, I think one dash at max is okay. Anything over one dash begins to appear low class, like a spam website. The GoDaddy link located on the last page of this book allows you to get your first domain name for only $0.99 for the first year. After that, the domain is $12 per year.

After you buy a domain name, you will need to buy a hosting plan. In simple terms, a "host" is the company that allows your website to appear on the internet. The web is basically a network of thousands and thousands of data servers. A hosting company has data servers where they store your website, which allows it to connect to the worldwide web. The hosting company I currently use is called Bluehost, and their service is only $3.95 a month (**fastlink.xyz/bluehost**). There are a lot of different hosting companies, and I have been through a few, however I have had the best experience with Bluehost. The main issue I had with other companies is my websites would randomly go down for hours at a time with no explanation. I have not had that problem with Bluehost. They have 24 hour tech support which is quite nice, and are very easy to work with. Bluehost also allows unlimited domain names to be stored on your account for one price. So whether you have 100 websites or just 1, you'll pay the same price each month.

GoDaddy also provides hosting. GoDaddy, like Bluehost, has 24 hour customer service and is a reliable provider. They are one of the biggest names on the internet. Using them for your domain name and hosting may make things easier for you, considering everything is in one place. There is also a link on the last page which provides GoDaddy hosting for $1 a month. So with a $0.99 domain name and $1 a month hosting, you're looking at $13 for the first year of your website. Not too bad!

There are a variety of tools available now a days to build websites, many of which require little to no coding knowledge. GoDaddy and Bluehost both have website builders. While this is an option, I would highly recommend at least knowing basic HTML and CSS. These two coding languages are the main building blocks of most websites and will be quite beneficial to know.

The most basic way to build a website is to start from scratch using a program like Dreamweaver or Microsoft Web Expressions; this is also the hardest way. I've found the easiest way to build websites is an online program called Wordpress. Every major hosting company provides a "Wordpress Installer," which allows you to install Wordpress automatically into your website. Wordpress was originally meant for blogging, but it has morphed into one of the main website design options for many different websites on the internet today.

Wordpress is extremely helpful to newbies because there are so many free features the program includes. It has hundreds and hundreds of free website templates you can use. With templates, the whole website is already designed for you. Then all you need to do is fill it in with your own info, and wholla, you have a website up and running. There are also templates you can pay for which can sometimes be beneficial depending on the website you are building. I've paid for templates myself and most go for around $50. This is a one-time payment, so not too expensive at all.

I am providing a Wordpress sales page template for free as a thank you for purchasing this book. Just email me at tim@unknownwealth.com and put "Sales Template" in the subject line, and I'll send it to you.

Wordpress has become a large community of different developers, and Wordpress sites can use what are called "plugins." You could think of these like apps for your phone. An iPhone can make calls, text, etc.

but apps allow it to do much more. It's the same way with your website and plugins. Some examples of plugin features include tracking visitor counts, stopping spam comments, embedding forms, etc. Many of these plugins are also free.

In terms of how to design your website, I would recommend looking at similar websites and emulating them. Look for big time gurus in the field who are selling eBooks on their website and try to create a similar design. Their website can be totally unrelated to the product you're selling, but that doesn't matter; you are just looking for ways to style your website. There is no reason to reinvent the wheel here. They've probably already done all the marketing research to figure out what works, what leads to conversions, etc. so why not just use their research to your advantage.

In terms of learning how to build websites, I learned two ways. The first way was by scouring the web and essentially teaching myself. I watched YouTube videos, read Google articles, bought books, and was able to figure out much of what I needed from studying and trial and error. I would not advise this method of learning as it's quite time consuming and there are quicker ways to learn. At the time though, in 2010, there wasn't as many helpful options on the internet as there are today.

Nowadays there are quite a few websites that will teach you web design and you can learn fairly quickly. One website that comes to mind is Udemy. I did not use this website when I got started, only because I didn't know about it, but I wish I did. This site is basically an online college, except the professors are self-proclaimed gurus in the field. You pay for their "class," which can range from $1-$200+, and you learn what the course is on. I'm actually currently using this website to learn how to build apps. And while I can't give you a direct recommendation on a web design course to take, I know there are a ton of high quality instructors teaching these courses on Udemy. Many times this website has sales where all courses are only $10. Do a quick google search before buying a class to see if the website has any coupon codes or sales running.

The second way I learned how to build websites was by actually taking a web design course in college. I was in college, majoring in Business at the time, and a certain computer science course titled "web design" caught my eye. I had been building websites for about 6 months prior to this and wanted to learn more about the subject. I'm glad I took the course as it was actually quite beneficial and corrected many of the errors I was making in my self-taught code. Depending on your current situation will determine if this is an option for you, or if taking an online course on a website like Udemy would be better.

Two other great websites to check out for learning web design are StackSkills.com and CodeAcademy.com. Stackskills is like Udemy, except more filtered towards computer and technology courses. CodeAcademy is a website offering free courses in many different programming languages.

After your website is built, you will need to put a price on the eBook you're selling. Ebooks generally go for between $30-$40, while some authors charge $70 or more. There is a fine line between making the most profit and what you charge for your book. The price you charge depends mostly on the information contained in your eBook and what your visitors are willing to pay for it. If you're selling a book on how to get rid of hiccups, then I'd say $3 would be a fair price. If you're selling a book on how to make money in the stock market, $100 or more would be fair. Most people with hiccups would just wait it out before they paid $100 for a book. And though you may get a few more sales selling your "stock" book for only $3, you may not make as much as if you had sold it for a $100. You may also lose a few sales as your intended audience may view your book as "cheap" and "not informative" at such a low price. This is why there is a fine line as I mentioned before.

To sell an eBook on your website, you will need some type of shopping cart system which sells your book for you, as well as delivers the eBook to the customer after they purchase it. I currently use a company called E-Junkie to take care of this for me. I've used E-Junkie since I got started selling eBooks and have had a great experience with them. They charge just $5 a month to sell and distribute up to ten eBooks.

Option #2: eBook Marketplace

The second option you have for selling your book is in an eBook marketplace. While the Amazon Kindle store would be considered the most popular option for this, there are quite a few other eBook marketplaces out there. I will be referring to the Amazon Kindle store during this book as that is the only eBook marketplace I have experience with.

There is definitely some allure to this option versus a website. You write your book, put it in the Kindle Store and bam, money starts rolling in. Well not that easily, but you get the idea. There is no website to build, no learning curve, and most everything is done for you. The only thing you really need to worry about is marketing your book. If you are in a low competition niche, your book may end up on the first page of Amazon by itself and additional marketing may not even be needed.

Amazon charges sellers a fee for each book sold in their marketplace. For books priced between $2.99 - $9.99, the fee is 30%. So if you sell your book for $2.99, Amazon would get 90 cents. Quite a hefty charge, but unfortunately it gets a little worse. If you sell your book for $10 or more, Amazon takes a 70% commission of the sale. So if you were to price your book at $10 and it sold, you would only make $3. They do this to keep the prices of eBooks down for their customers. This is good for the consumer, but not so much for the seller.

This means, for the most part, your books on Amazon will sell in the range of $2.99 - $9.99. While this may not seem like much, a few hundred books selling at $4.99 is pretty nice. And that's just with one book. If you write 2 or 3 or 4 books, you now have money flowing in from more directions. And that $4.99 a few hundred times has now become $19.96 a few hundred times with the four books you are selling.

There are quite a few notable authors who do very well for themselves in the Kindle store. One that comes to mind is named Patrick King. He focuses on one subject with his books, and that is human psychology. He has quite a few books for sale in the Kindle store and while they vary slightly, they are all related to human psychology. So if you're knowledgeable about a particular subject, you don't have to stop at one book in that category.

One reason writing more than one book in the same category is beneficial is because of the additional revenue it can bring you. Customers who come to the Kindle store tend to buy more than one book, whether it be at that moment or in the future. There is a section below each book description titled "Customers Who Bought This Book Also Bought." This section lists about five other books which are frequently purchased with the book currently being viewed. Many times other books you have written, related to the same subject, will show up in this section. Amazon does this because it generates more sales. So if you don't have another book in this section, you're missing out on sales.

Another reason you may gain additional sales is because customers like your book and want to read more books you have written. To do this, they'll navigate to your Kindle store page which lists all the books you have for sale on Amazon. If you don't have any more books on this page, you're again missing out on potential sales.

Of course your books do not need to all be on the same subject, this is just one strategy to consider. The real key is the more books you have out in the Kindle store, and marketed effectively, the more potential income you will generate.

If writing books on more than one subject, a good idea is to use pen names. The reason for this is the author looks more reputable if her name is associated with one subject versus a slew of them. People put more trust in someone when it looks like they're an expert in one subject, versus just trying to sell products in everything. So if you decide to write books in the subjects of psychology and dog training, one of the books should include your real name, and the other a pen name you come up with. Or you can just use two pen names. Either way, make sure to associate one name with one book subject.

Now that you know a little bit more about selling your book, let's go through the steps, from start to finish, of how to get your book in the Kindle Store. First, you obviously have to write the book. This can be done in Microsoft Word. When writing your book in Word, you want to make sure you include a few things:

1. A cover page. This can be done by clicking the "insert" tab at the top, and then clicking "cover page."

2. A table of contents page. This can be done by clicking the "reference" tab at the top of the page, and then clicking "Table of Contents."

3. A header or a footer which includes the title of the book, and the page number.

4. When writing new chapters, make sure to click "Heading 1" at the top of the page. This allows the table of contents to recognize that you are starting a new chapter. You can edit the "Heading 1" settings by right-clicking on it, or command clicking on a Mac.

5. At the end of each chapter, use a "page break." This is for proper formatting when viewed on a Kindle device. This can be done by clicking the "insert" tab at the top of the page, and then clicking "page break."

Next you're going to need to make a cover for your book. You want a 2D image which will be used as the book's picture in the Kindle Store. You can also make a rear page, like paperback books have, with a description you have written. While not necessary, it can make your book look more professional and increase sales.

Now some people are able to do the graphic design themselves, however most people do not have this skill. When I first got started, I tried doing a Google search for graphic designers and found many charging hundreds of dollars just to design a book cover! That is where the website called Fiverr which I had mentioned before comes in. Here you are able to find graphic designers willing to make an eBook cover for only $5! These aren't novices either; these are talented designers that make great covers! I've had quite a few covers designed using Fiverr and I've been happy with all of them. Just look at the reviews of the designer before you decide to choose him or her.

There is also a way to make a nice looking cover yourself. There is a website called Canva.com. This website provides layouts for anything graphic design you can think of: posters, flyers, letters, and yes, book covers! You only have to pay if you use one of the images they provide on the website, and most go for only a $1. So this is another very inexpensive way for you to design your book cover.

After you have written your book and designed your cover, you will want to convert it into Kindle format (kpf) and observe how it will look to your readers. To do this, you want to download a free program called Kindle Create which can be found here: **fastlink.xyz/kindle**

This program is offered by Amazon, and puts the book in the correct format so it is displayed correctly on e-readers, Kindles, iPads, etc. Technically you could upload a Microsoft Word document onto Kindle Store without using Kindle Create, but many times it will be jumbled around with improper spacing, sizing, etc. which looks unsightly to potential customers and could greatly hurt your product reviews.

Once you have written your book, converted it in Kindle Create, and verified it is formatted correctly, it is time to upload it to the Kindle Store. After you convert the book with Kindle Create, it places the kindle book into an output folder. This folder is where you get the book when you upload it to the Kindle store.

When the book uploads to the Kindle store, you will need to decide on a book title, write a description for your book, and upload your eBook cover image.

The title and description of your eBook are very important aspects to consider. The title and description are one of the main factors when it comes to whether or not your book shows up in the search results. For this reason, you want to include keyword phrases with a large number of customer searches in your book description. I am not aware of any tool currently available that lets you see the number of searches for a particular keyword phrase on Amazon. There is however, a viable alternative. In the next chapter, I talk more about the "Keyword Planner" tool which is in Google Adwords. This tool allows you to see the number of Google searches per month for any particular keyword phrase you type in. It also gives you suggestions of more keyword phrases you can target. Google Adwords is the advertising side of Google, where you can buy ads that are displayed in the Google search engine.

While the number of searches on Google and Amazon may not be identical, the Keyword Planner tool can give you a good idea of how many people are interested in a particular subject, and should correlate well into number of searches for a keyword phrase on Amazon. You want to use this tool to gain insight into the most popular searches correlated with the book you're selling. We may assume we know what the most popular search terms are without actually being correct. Sometimes even slight differences in wording can have an impact when showing in search results.

Once you've decided on search phrases you plan on targeting, you want to try and fit a few of these in your Kindle book title and description. This is so people who use different search phrases will end up seeing your book in their search results. And you of course want it to look natural. You only need to place a keyword phrase in your description once, as repeating it is a waste of space and will not bring about better results on your book's search ranking. Using similes of words throughout your description is a good idea. So if you're selling a book on teaching parrots to talk, you could put "teach your parrot to talk" somewhere and "get your bird to speak" somewhere else. This gives your book a better chance of ranking if someone types in bird, instead of parrot, or speak, instead of talk, in the search box. Make sure your description is long and well filled out. Use all the boxes and blank space they give you; the more the better in my opinion.

Another item that will benefit your description is having a list of bullet style sales snippets. These are short sentences with benefits the customer will receive if they buy your book. Examples include "Find out the quickest way to get your parrot talking in Chapter 2," "Learn how to teach your parrot another language on page 45," and so on. These are potential benefits the customer could be searching for, and will make them more likely to buy your book.

Something to note is the description section text is editable with HTML. This is a coding language which allows you to make words bold, large, bulleted, etc. The list of HTML approved symbols Amazon allows you to use can be found here: **fastlink.xyz/html**

While your book description is of course important, it's even more beneficial if you have the main keyword phrase you're focusing on in the title of your book. You have a better chance of appearing in the search results if the keyword phrase is in the title. A good way to do this is to place it in the subtitle. So with the same premise of an eBook on teaching parrots to talk, an example of a good book title would be "Chatty Cathy: How to Teach Your Parrot to Talk."

Once you have your book uploaded and into the Kindle store, you can begin marketing it which I detail in the next chapter.

CHAPTER 4
Marketing Your eBook

_____

Marketing your eBook correlates with how well you are able to sell products. There are many books on the art of selling. Some good ones include "Spin Selling" and "The Challenger Sale." While reading the whole book may be more beneficial, reading book summaries can save a tremendous amount of time. Websites like Sparknotes and Cliffnotes are good places to start, but many times they do not have the particular book you may be searching for. A quick Google search such as "spin selling summary" brings up a host of websites which provide a book summary for you. These are usually free, to the point, and can save you quite a bit of time learning what is presented in the book.

Now, let's go over the different platforms where you can market your eBook.

Option #1: Your Own Website

Before you get started marketing your eBook on your own website, you want to set up Google Analytics and Google Webmaster Tools. These two free Google tools allow you to see a ton of information regarding your website that is quite beneficial when it comes to collecting data. Let's go over some of the features of these tools.

Visitor Count – this allows you to see the number of visitors coming to your website on a daily basis.

Bounce Rate – shows the number of visitors who are entering your website, and then immediately leaving because they don't like what they see.

Search Phrases – shows the main search phrases that visitors are using to find your website.

Backlinks – displays the websites that have hyperlinks pointing from their site to yours.

Errors – checks for errors within your site that prevents it from showing up in Google.

These are just a few of the features Google Analytics and Google Webmaster Tools offer. There are many more features which are quite beneficial when making a website. So make sure to sign up for these free tools as soon as you get started.

There are three primary methods to marketing an eBook via a website. They include:

1. Pay-Per Click Advertising (PPC)
2. Search Engine Optimization (SEO)
3. Affiliate Marketing

Pay-Per Click (PPC) Advertising - Google

When you search on Google, you'll notice ads on the top and side of the screen. These are advertisers who are paying Google to show up in search results for certain keywords visitors type on the search engine. How this process works is a visitor types in a search phrase on Google and an ad is displayed. An advertiser is only charged if the visitor clicks on their link, which is why it is called "pay-per click." The cost of the click can vary depending on how competitive the keyword is you're targeting. While I am giving you a good idea of how to get started, I don't include all the fine details of Google Adwords in this book. If you decide to use the pay-per click method to market your eBook, I highly suggest you get a copy of the book titled "Ultimate Guide to Adwords" by Perry Marshall and Mike Rhodes (**fastlink.xyz/adwords**). This book goes over the best strategies to use on PPC advertising, and can greatly increase your conversion and click rate. I read this book when I first got started and it has tons and tons of helpful information that will allow you to run a successful pay-per-click campaign.

To get started with Google Adwords, you will need to open an Adwords account. There are quite a few coupons available on the web which give you $100 - $150 in free advertising spend when you sign up for an account. So I would highly suggest looking for one before you sign up.

There are other search engines you can run pay-per click campaigns on such as Yahoo and Bing, however I would recommend Google as your primary venue. This is because Google is the most popular search engine, with a market share of 65% of all searches on the internet. An eBook guru named Eben Pagen who I mentioned earlier strictly used pay-per click advertising to sell his eBook "Double Your Dating" and was highly successful with it. You have to find a profitable balance between the amount you pay per click, and the number of sales you receive for your eBook. Some big factors you want to consider with pay-per click advertising are:

- Keyword competition
- Cost per click (CPC)
- Price of the eBook you're selling

• Daily spend amount

If you have a competitive keyword, more than likely other advertisers will be in the search results with you. Google gives the top position in the search results to the advertiser who bids the most per click. So while one keyword phrase may have an extremely high volume of searches, it may not be worth it to bid on that keyword because of the high cost per click. Sometimes it's more beneficial to find many different long tail keywords you can bid on, which all have a lower CPC. I talk more about long tail keywords later on, but in essence they are longer, less competitive search phrases versus the shorter, more popular ones.

Depending on the price of your eBook will determine how much you want to spend per click. An eBook selling for $100 would be able to have a higher spend rate then one selling for $10. You will have to do some tests on your own in the beginning to determine how many clicks it takes on average to make a sale or conversion. Then, after you calculate your conversion rate, you can determine the amount you are willing to spend per day on ads. Google allows you to set a max daily spend, so they will stop displaying your ad after this limit is met. So you can never spend more than your "max daily spend" in any given day. You can also pause and delete Adwords campaigns in the case you want to take a break.

In order for PPC advertising to work effectively, the main thing you need to focus on is a strong conversion rate. This is the rate of customers who come to your website and buy your book, versus the ones who come to your website and leave. Customers decide within seconds of visiting a page if they want to stay or not, so it is imperative your site keeps their interest. You want to have what is known as a strong "above the fold" area on your website. Above the fold refers to the top part of your website before a user scrolls down the page, as that is the first thing they see when they view a webpage.

To keep them on the page, many eBook gurus are using a video which starts playing as soon as they visit the site. This video is used to explain your product and make the visitor want to scroll down the page and learn more about your book. One sales technique which works well with these videos is giving away a little piece of your book for free, so the visitor gets a taste and will want to learn more. So if you're selling an eBook on how to gain muscle, you could include a quick tip on how to gain muscle in your biceps and show this exercise in your video. Then you could explain why purchasing the book would be beneficial, and tell them to scroll down the page to learn more and buy the complete product.

While any video will help, currently whiteboard videos seem to be the preferred method with marketers. You have probably seen this type of video before, as it's quite popular. It's a video where it looks like someone is drawing on a whiteboard with a marker, and it's all animated. Here's a quick video link to one in case you're unfamiliar with what I'm referring to: **fastlink.xyz/whiteboard**

Fiverr has sellers who offer this service, however it can get a little pricey. Another option would be to make a live video, with yourself talking. This is the method Eben Pagen used to sell his eBook, "Double Your Dating." While this may have been pricey some time ago, nowadays it can be done fairly cheaply. Most people's phones have pretty great video cameras in this day and age, so you would just need to get a camera tripod to place the phone on, as well as an adapter which allows the phone to screw into the tripod. These adapters can easily be found on eBay for less than $5, and tripods go for less than $15. Then you will want to get a green screen. These go for about $30 on eBay, and this includes not just the screen but everything necessary to set it up, which includes the polls, stands, etc.

Another option is to make a PowerPoint video. This is the least expensive option, and is fairly easy to do. It is also the option I use for my websites. If you don't have much experience with PowerPoint, I would suggest watching the many YouTube videos on the subject. Let me give you a brief explanation on how to create an exciting PowerPoint video that will keep your customers on your website. For this video option, you will need to get a microphone if you don't already have one. A quality mic can be found on eBay and Amazon for less than $40.

You start off with a blank slide. On this first slide you want to add pictures, as well as a large bold title. This is the first text customers will see and hear when they visit your website. For this reason, you want it to stand out and really catch their attention so they will be interested in watching more of your video. Let's say you're selling a book on getting in shape. A nice bold title could be "Discover the Little Known Way to Get a Six Pack With This Easy Trick." Something that intrigues the customer, is a mystery to the customer. You want the customer to really think "I have to watch this video!"

Each corresponding slide should include text and pictures to continually engage the customer throughout the presentation. The microphone I referred to before will be used to voiceover your PowerPoint video while the text and pictures are displayed on the screen. On each slide you should include animations. Examples would be text fading in, an image shooting in from the side, expanding and retracting the text, etc. Basically an exciting video that continually keeps the user's attention. You can also include animations when transferring from one slide to the next. When you are finished making the video, you will click "File" → "Export" → "Create Video." This will save your video into an uploadable format which can then be placed on YouTube.

While I have put the video directly onto the backend of my website in the past, I find a better alternative is to upload the video to YouTube, and then embed the YouTube video into your website. The reason for this is download speed. As said before, you want the video to play immediately to get the visitors attention as soon as they visit your website. Many times when a video is directly uploaded to your website it takes time to load and can take quite a while before it begins playing. This is bad for conversions and customers will sometimes leave before the video even starts. When you embed the video from YouTube, it usually loads and plays much quicker.

Your most important concern when it comes to using Adwords should be the keywords you're targeting. This is where the Adwords "Keyword Planner Tool" comes in. This tool allows you to see the number of searches a particular keyword phrase gets per month, as well as the competition for that keyword. It also allows you to see the estimated cost per click you will be charged. This keyword tool will become invaluable in not just Adwords, but all your marketing endeavors.

While the most searched keywords will provide the most traffic to your website, sometimes the cost of them is so high your profit margin will be little, or even negative if you end up bidding on them. This is where something called "long tail keywords" come into play. Long tail keywords are keyword phrases that are longer than the more popular search terms. For this reason, they get less traffic on Google but are also usually much less expensive to bid on. So instead of bidding on one, high traffic keyword that costs a fortune per click, you can bid on multiple low traffic keywords that cost much less. All the long tail keywords combined can end up bringing you the same amount of traffic or more, than the one high traffic keyword.

So let's say you're selling a book on how to gain muscle. A very popular, expensive keyword would be "gain muscle." A long tail keyword, which would be less expensive, would be "what is the best way to gain muscle fast" or "strategies to gain the most muscle." These longer tail keywords also give you more targeted customers who are definitely searching for a strategy which correlates with your eBook. The

Adwords keyword tool has a ton of search suggestions which can help give you ideas when deciding on keywords to target. You can also do a Google search with a keyword that relates to your eBook and then scroll down to the bottom of the page. Here Google has a number of suggestions which can also be used as keywords to focus on.

When using Adwords, you want to make sure to include the search phrase in the title of your ad, and the body. When a user searches for a phrase and your ad appears, the entered phrase will be shown in bold in your ad. This correlates with a higher click rate for your ad. More tips like this are mentioned in the book "Ultimate Guide to Adwords" which I mentioned earlier.

Pay-Per Click Advertising - Facebook

Another PPC advertiser you can use is Facebook. Facebook is a different marketing strategy than Google. With Google, users are typing in a search and looking for something specific. On Facebook, you're putting an ad in front of the user and trying to get them to click on it. So you could, in theory, get a lot more people to look at your product. This is because they may not have been interested or even knew about your product before, but when your ad appears they want to learn more.

What's nice about Facebook is you can target your ad down to the finest detail in terms of who it's shown to. You can target by sex, age, race, etc. So if you have a product meant for teenagers, you can exclude the ad from showing to adults. This can save you money from unwarranted clicks on your ad.

Similar to Adwords, creating a quality ad that gets clicks is a lot harder than just throwing a few words and a picture together. There is a lot of strategy and technique behind it. For this reason, I highly suggest you get a hold of "Ultimate Guide to Facebook Marketing" (**fastlink.xyz/facebook**). It's made by the same company that makes "Ultimate Guide to Adwords" and is equally as helpful. This book teaches you all the strategy you will need to know for creating successful Facebook marketing campaigns for your eBook. It's extremely beneficial and I would not start advertising on Facebook without it.

Search Engine Optimization (SEO)

This is by far my favorite way to market eBooks, and the primary method I use. In this day and age users are more likely to click on organic search results versus what they suspect is an ad, as it appears more trustworthy in their eyes. The numbers say organic listing receive 90% of the clicks, compared to 10% for advertisements. This method of marketing is the most expensive, however the amount spent ends up paying off generously in the long run. Search Engine Optimization (SEO) is a fairly detailed subject, so I can only touch on the subject briefly in this book, as it's a whole course in itself. I would highly suggest picking up a copy of "SEO for Dummies" or taking a course on Udemy which goes over the subject in a lot more detail. Even if you end up hiring someone to do this for you, you need to have an understanding of the subject for your own reference.

With SEO, the two most important factors which influence where your website ranks on search engines are:

1. Website Content
2. Backlinks

Let's go over these.

Website content is a big deal in Google's eyes, and rightly so. They are looking to display websites which correlate most to what their visitors are searching for. So the more related your website is to the search term typed on Google, the more likely it will show in the search results. There are many other fine details when Google evaluates website content besides just the words on the page. This includes things like text that is in bold, the amount of times text is displayed, text in H1 tags, etc. This is all explained in "SEO for Dummies."

The next factor is called "backlinks." Backlinks are just when other websites have links on their page, which point to your website. More backlinks result in a higher search result ranking in Google. In the past, all you had to do was get a ton of spammy websites to link to your site, and you could easily get your website on the first page of Google for any keyword phrase you wanted. This is no longer the case. Nowadays it's quality over quantity. Google is looking for sites with backlinks coming from quality websites which share a topic related to the domain. The more important and well-respected a website, the more significant a link coming from it means to Google. If the homepage of Yahoo has a link on it pointing to your website, this is much more significant than a link from Joe Blow's blog. And thus, your website would gain a much bigger boost in its search engine ranking position (SERP).

Another new feature Google has introduced is something known as the "Google Sandbox." When a domain is brand new, Google puts it on a probationary period before it ranks well for its intended keywords. This "Google Sandbox" usually lasts between 1-6 months. The reason for this is because in the past, people could make spam websites, get them to rise quickly by buying backlinks and ruin the search results quality for Google users. Google would then have to ban the website from its search engine, but the website operator could just make a new domain and do it all again. So, in essence, Google is making sure the website deserves to be in their search engine with the probationary period they place it on.

Because of this "Google Sandbox," you want to buy your domain name as soon as possible. Then, by the time you're done writing your eBook and creating your website, enough time should have gone by to where you are no longer affected by this issue.

Due to the many different Google algorithms which determine a website's rank, SEO can take a long time. Even with a very experienced SEO company, just seeing your website appear somewhere in Google can take weeks. Actually getting to the first page can take between 4-6 months, or even longer. The amount of time it takes depends on the competition for the keyword you're targeting. All search phrases have competing websites which are trying to get that 1st page spot on Google. The first page of Google is the holy grail in search land, and the only place where you can really expect to get sales. Less than 10% of searchers even go past the 1st page, so the chance of getting a sale reduces dramatically if your site is on page 2 or beyond.

SEO is an art in itself. No one knows the true algorithms which Google uses to rank websites, though we have a good idea. You can do SEO yourself, however it's incredibly time consuming as well as quite difficult for the lay person. It's also an ongoing process and isn't just stopped when you get to page one. You have to keep getting backlinks and maintain your rankings while you're there. So while I would highly suggest learning about SEO, doing it yourself is out of the question in my opinion.

Ninety-nine percent of the time, with SEO companies, cheaper is not better. Many companies overseas and in India charge $50 - $150 a month for SEO, but don't be enticed by their low prices; they often do very little if anything, and at the end of 6 months your website is still not in the search results. Then when you try to apply for the "money back guarantee" they offer, they stop replying to your emails and calls. I used a few of these companies when I first got started and definitely regret it. The lowest you should expect to pay for quality SEO is $500 a month. This may seem like a lot, but if you have a good product and website, you can easily make your money back once you start ranking well on Google. The number of daily sales you can get varies greatly depending on the demand for your product and the number of searches per day on Google for keywords your website appears under.

Let's say after 6 months you're ranking on the first page of Google and people are starting to buy your eBook. You are getting 3 book sales a day for $30 a book. The math would be:

$30 x 3 books a day = $90
$90 x 30 days in a month = $2,700
$2,700 - $500 for SEO = $2,200

And three books a day is just random, as it does vary greatly. I've sold 5 books in one day many times.

If you are really tight on money, Fiverr and Upwork do have sellers offering SEO services for quite low prices. On Fiverr you can even find SEO services for just $5! The quality of SEO on these sites varies greatly with the different sellers, so the main concern is finding someone who can deliver. The best way I've found to do this is with keyword tests. Take two, long tail keywords which are similar in terms of number of searches per month and competitiveness (this can be found with the Keyword Planner tool in Google Adwords). Have one seller perform SEO services on the first keyword, and another seller perform SEO services on the second. Then after a month has gone by, check on where you're keywords are ranking on Google. The higher the seller got the keyword in the search results, the better he is. You can do these tests with a variety of different sellers to see who the best is. Finding someone who is good at SEO on these websites is like finding gold. This is because, as I stated before, the price of SEO with regular companies is quite expensive, so you'd be paying a fraction of the cost.

If you decide to use an actual company, just know smaller SEO companies are usually the best bet. This is because the smaller companies have more to lose when losing a customer. Many times they are only working on a few SEO projects at a time, and will work harder to make sure you stay with them. A bigger company has much less to lose if one of their clients leave them. In my experience, large SEO companies are all talk and rarely deliver.

Something else to note is many times SEO companies can pop up and go out of business within months. This is because of the ease of getting into the business. You just need a website, phone number, and an email. So don't take their word for it when they tell you they can rank your website on page 1. Check how long they've been in business, how long they've used the same domain name, reviews on Google, and ask for examples of websites they're currently ranking. A reputable company will be happy to provide you with all this information. Know too that price is always negotiable with SEO. So negotiate, as you will most likely be able to get a better price than what they first offer you, or have listed on their website.

While a company is running an SEO campaign for you, they should keep you updated at the minimum monthly, with how your targeted keywords are ranking in Google. You can check this yourself though by using a Search Engine Ranking Position (SERP) tool. A SERP tool shows you where the keyword phrases you are targeting for your website are ranking in Google. There are quite a few websites, as well as Chrome and Firefox extensions, which offer this service. This is very beneficial to have when using an SEO company, to verify what they're telling you matches what you are able to see yourself.

Affiliate Marketing

Affiliate marketing is when you promote someone else's product, and then get a cut of the sale. You could think of an affiliate marketer as a casting agent. The agent promotes an actor and then when the actor gets cast for a role in a movie, the agent gets a cut of their paycheck. Affiliate marketing is a big deal in the eBook world and something I did in the beginning of my career. Some people do very well strictly being affiliate marketers without any product of their own. Personally, I feel it's much more profitable to be the one who actually writes the book than it is to be the one just trying to sell it.

Affiliate marketers are a great resource to have when promoting your eBook. The best website I've found for this is called Clickbank. This website has a ton of affiliate marketers who are looking to promote eBooks, as they get a cut of each sale. This takes all the time and money out of marketing the book yourself, as other people are doing it for you. I do not currently use Clickbank, as I do the marketing myself, but that is just my personal preference. Some eBook authors strictly use Clickbank and do none of the marketing themselves. Clickbank takes 40% of whatever you sell your book for. So if you sell your book for $30, you only end up making $18. While 40% is a big piece of the pie, the amount you spend in marketing could end up being more than 40%, so you need to decide which is a better route for yourself. As mentioned, I don't use this method but many eBook gurus do. One notable author who uses this strategy is named Michael Fiore. He's written quite a few books, and currently has a popular one titled "Text Your Ex Back." Michael has been featured on the Rachel Ray show, and is pretty famous in the eBook world.

Option #2: eBook Marketplace

Marketing your book in the Kindle store is a bit different than the types of marketing we have gone over so far. One advantage to the Amazon Kindle store is, unlike the other forms of marketing we have talked about (PPC and SEO), once the book ends up on the first page and customers start buying it, it starts to market itself. At that point you can stop spending your marketing dollars on that particular eBook and can start marketing another one. This strategy can build regular recurring income that lasts.

Like Google, if your book is not on the first page of search results in Amazon, the number of sales drops dramatically. This is because many customers don't go past the first page when looking for a book. One important factor Amazon considers when showing a book in their search results is if the keyword phrase can be found in your title and/or description. Other factors include customer review score, the number of customer reviews, the number of book purchases, and the total revenue the author has received from the book.

High book conversion rates are all about quality and professionalism. You need to have a quality title, description, and eBook cover so people respect your book and are more likely to purchase it. The book itself needs to be written well, in the correct Kindle format, and free of spelling and grammatical errors. This all adds up to higher star reviews for your book, which then increases your rank and sales.

Amazon does allow you to promote your book as a "sponsored listing." This is similar to Google's pay-per click advertising. Your book will display on the first page of search results and when someone clicks on it, Amazon charges you a small fee. This is a great strategy to use when just starting out with no reviews.

Reviews are key to getting more purchases. Like getting a job with no experience, getting purchases with no reviews is quite tough. One option you have is buying reviews. Amazon frowns upon this greatly, and the reviews will be removed immediately if you get caught. Do a Google search and you'll see quite a bit of people selling reviews on Amazon. These "bought reviews" can be quite expensive, but they do end up paying off in the long run. Even if you buy just 3 reviews, this can help you get that first real customer to buy your book and propel your sales. I do not buy reviews, nor do I advocate it, but I do let you know it's an option some people use.

Another option to obtain reviews when first getting started is to give away your book for free. In the past you used to be able to offer customers incentives such as gift cards, prizes, etc. to leave reviews on your book.

This quickly got abused though and Amazon did away with this option. The only allowable thing Amazon now allows is giving your book away free.

If you're not showing up on the first page for your desired keyword, I would not hesitate to both pay for a sponsored listing and give your book away for free. This will bring in the customer reviews you desperately need. Though you will lose a little money in the beginning, this strategy will pay off generously in the long run. And as mentioned before, once your book has begun ranking on the first page, more people will buy it and leave reviews and it becomes a recurring cycle. You no longer have to pay for sponsored listings or buy reviews, and the book begins marketing itself. There are some Amazon customers who scourer the "top free" books each week and download and read whatever they can get their hands on. Typically books which are on the high end of these lists get more downloads. More downloads = more sales = higher rankings = possibly more reviews. For this reason, in the beginning list your book in obscure categories so you rise to the top, as many other free books will not be there. Change your book back to the proper category when your free book promotion is over. When you are giving your book away for free, a good idea is to have a review "network." This could include co-workers, friends, etc. You can ask these people to buy the book (for free) and then leave an honest review. Just one review on a book looks much better than zero reviews. For this reason, just getting a few people from your network to leave a quality review on your book can have profound impacts on your sales, which will in turn get you more reviews in the future.

On average, 1/1000 customers typically leave a review on books. For this reason, place bold text throughout your book thanking your customer for reading your book, and asking them nicely to leave a review. You can also include a link to the review page, making it that much easier for them. Reviews are the backbone to getting sales on Amazon, and this will help remind your customers to leave you a review.

I want you to think about sometime too. Just 1/1000 customers typically leave a review. There are books on Amazon with thousands of reviews. Considering this, I want you to think about how many books that person has sold to get that many reviews... millions. This can be you too!

Additional Products to Sell

While eBooks are one information product you can sell on the internet, there are others that can provide additional income. I would suggest writing one book, and then converting it into the additional products I specify below. Some people don't have kindle readers, or maybe they don't want to buy an eBook. There is a whole slew of customers who prefer books and information in different formats, and you are missing out on sales if you don't offer your book in them. All you're doing is taking your book which is already written, and converting it to a different format. All the work is already done, yet it's like your selling many more products. Here are some options for you.

Video Course

A video course is a great way to gain additional income. I mentioned a website called Udemy earlier in the book where you could go to learn web design; well Udemy can also be used for you to make money.

You can sign up as an instructor on Udemy and then make courses in video format. To do this, you would just need to turn your eBook into a video. This can be done by using PowerPoint. I mentioned using PowerPoint before to make explainer videos on your website. It would be a similar process, just with a longer video detailing your whole book. You can have a video of yourself talking in parts of your course, pictures with voiceovers, animations on the screen, etc. I would advise looking at videos other sellers have made to get a good idea of what one of these courses look like. If you've bought a course on Udemy, that is one place to get an idea. You can also look at the trailer that many Udemy courses provide for free, or you can go on YouTube to find informational videos. These can all be used to give you a better idea on how to make a video to start your own course on Udemy.

Similar to the Kindle Store, once the video starts getting reviews and getting more purchases, the higher it moves up in the rankings. Your video course becomes residual income that you receive day in and day out. You can be running an SEO campaign for your own website while also providing a course on Udemy. You could even offer the book in the Kindle store at the same time. You now have multiple revenue streams of passive income all stemming from the same product, just in different venues.

eBay

With eBay you don't even have to do any converting! Your book is written. Just make sure it's in PDF format you're good to go. Though you will most likely get fewer product sales on eBay versus other venues, this is just one more way to bring in residual income. So say you make just one sale a week on eBay; that's one sale a week you would have been missing out on. With eBay, listing an item is free, you only pay a small fee when it sells. There is also no shipping, as you can just send the customer a link to your product using the E-Junkie service I spoke of earlier in the book. So there really is no downside to using eBay as another outlet to sell your book.

Paperback Book

Amazon makes selling a paperback book easier than ever. Years ago to sell a paperback book, you had to order a minimum of 2,000 copies from a book publisher which was very expensive, and then hope your books sold and ship them out yourself. This is no longer the case. With Amazon, you do not have to worry about getting the book "published" as Amazon does this for you, as they have paperback book printers at all their facilities. This means you do not have to put out the funds to order thousands of copies of your paperback book to get started. Amazon makes and ships paperback books "on-demand" which means as soon as someone orders your paperback book, it's printed and shipped out at an Amazon facility. This means you don't even have to ship the book yourself, as Amazon does this for you too! The whole process is literally hands off. You upload your book to Amazon, it gets approved, and then you don't touch it ever again.

The paperback book is a little different from a kindle book. First, the margins have to be different because of how the text is printed and the book is placed together. You can find margin templates which correspond to Microsoft Word on the Amazon website here: **fastlink.xyz/template**

Second, you have to upload the correctly formatted paperback version of your book to your Kindle Direct Publishing account. The book can be in .docx or .pdf format and you upload it alongside your kindle book at kdp.amazon.com. You are even given the option to make a stand alone paperback book in the case you don't want to offer a kindle version, however I wouldn't recommend that.

Third is the cover. This cover has to be edited to fit correctly when being printed. There is also a back cover on a paperback book. While some others leave this blank, I highly recommend placing some text which gives a highlight of your book. This makes it appear more professional. This editing process is not too tough if you know how to use Photoshop or

Paint.net. If you don't, the website Fiverr offers this service. Here is the templates for paperback versions of covers from Amazon: **fastlink.xyz/paperback**

The default version for paperback books Amazon sets is 6" x 9" with a matte finish. Usually this is too big for most books, so I recommend changing the settings to 5" x 8" when uploading your book. I also recommend changing the finish to "glossy," as this appears more professional than matte. Amazon charges higher fees for a paperback book, so most sellers charge a higher price for the paperback version versus the Kindle version.

Audiobook

Audiobooks are yet another way to pile on sales to your eBook. This is quite an easy way to make additional income as well. You have already written the book, at this point you just need to record yourself reading it. Some people may not have the best voice for narrating an audiobook. This is another service that the website I love, Fiverr, offers. Quite a few sellers offer a "book narrating" service and they have outstanding voices. The price varies depending on the length of the book, but you can expect to pay about $200. While this may seem like a lot at first, this is a small price to pay to have yet another product making you residual income indefinitely. You can place your new audiobook in the Amazon Kindle store right alongside your eBook. This will not only bring you in additional revenue, it also makes your product appear more professional, which could potentially generate more sales.

The website you upload your audiobook to is ADX.com. ADX then links your audiobook to your kindle version so they both appear on the Amazon page.

If you want to record the book yourself and feel you have sufficient skills using the audio editing software Audacity, this can be a cheaper option. A quality recording microphone on Amazon goes for around $30. I've had a better experience with USB microphones, as the 3.5mm jack ones have more background noise. Just know that a bad sounding audiobook will get you negative reviews, so make sure the sound is clear and your words are spoken clearly before uploading it to ACX.

Multiple Languages

English is my native language, as it may be yours as well. There are 7 billion people in the world, many of whom don't speak English. English is actually third on the list, with Chinese and Spanish topping it. Considering the number of people who do not speak English, they are not able to understand your book and thus are not going to buy it. You already have your book written, why not get it translated into another language? This is just one more revenue stream for residual income from just one single book. Many people know someone who speaks another language. I'm sure if you negotiate with them and offer them a little money, they'd be more than happy to translate your book. You can also use the website Fiverr for book translators.

Customer Reviews

⭐⭐⭐⭐⭐ 38

4.8 out of 5 stars ▾

5 star	████████	87%
4 star	█	10%
3 star		3%
2 star		0%
1 star		0%

See all 38 customer reviews ›

Share your thoughts with other customers

Write a customer review

If you are enjoying this book, could you please leave a review on Amazon? It would be greatly appreciated and allow me to come out with more informative books in the future. A shortened link to the review page is below:

fastlink.xyz/make

Conclusion

I hope you enjoyed the book and learned a wealth of information from it. Getting started can take a little time, but you should now have the tools and knowledge to get you there much faster. Even doing this part time can add a nice chunk of change each week to your pocket. There is of course no limit to the amount of money you can make using this strategy as the more books you write, the more you can make. As I mentioned before, there are quite a few people who have become millionaires from eBooks. Now that you have the knowledge and tools to do it, you could be next. I wish you the best in your endeavors!

Note: Links to all websites mentioned in this book can be found on the last page.

If you enjoyed this book, you may also like:

The Crash Signal
The One Signal That Predicts a Stock Market Crash

Shortened Link to Amazon Page:
fastlink.xyz/crash

If you know anything about the stock market, you know crashes are inevitable... but losing money in those crashing doesn't have to be! In this book, Tim Morris shows you the one signal which has flashed before every stock market crash for the last 60 years! Will you be prepared for the next crash? Save your money before it's too late with The Crash Signal!

How to Make an Audiobook
For Amazon, iTunes, and Audible

Shortened Link to Amazon Page:
fastlink.xyz/audiobook

Have a great kindle book you want your customers to be able to listen to? Want to earn extra income from your books? This can all be done by making an audiobook! In this book Rob Branson shows you everything you need to know, from start to finish, on how to make an audiobook. Look professional and stand out from your competition. Learn how to make an audiobook now!

How to Publish a Book

Your Complete Guide on How to Self-Publish a Kindle & Paperback Book on Amazon

Shortened Link to Amazon Page:

fastlink.xyz/publish

Amazon has made becoming an author easier than ever! Now you too can make a Kindle & paperback book & have it selling within 24 hours! In this book, Rob Branson shows you exactly how to go from your rough draft to your finished, uploaded product. It's the smoothest guide out there on how to make a book. Find out more at the link above!

WEBSITE LINKS

**Note: Some of these links contain coupon codes which can save you a significant amount of money versus going to the website directly.

Udemy - **fastlink.xyz/udemy**

Upwork - **fastlink.xyz/upwork**

CodeAcademy - **fastlink.xyz/code**

StackSkills - **fastlink.xyz/stack**

E-Junkie - **fastlink.xyz/junkie**

GoDaddy - **fastlink.xyz/godaddy**

Fiverr - **fastlink.xyz/fiver**

Bluehost - **fastlink.xyz/bluehost**

Clickbank - **fastlink.xyz/clickbank**